The Urbana Free Library

To renew: call **217-367-4057**
or go to **urbanafreelibrary.org**
and select **My Account**

THEN AND NOW
COMMUNICATION THEN AND NOW

by Nadia Higgins

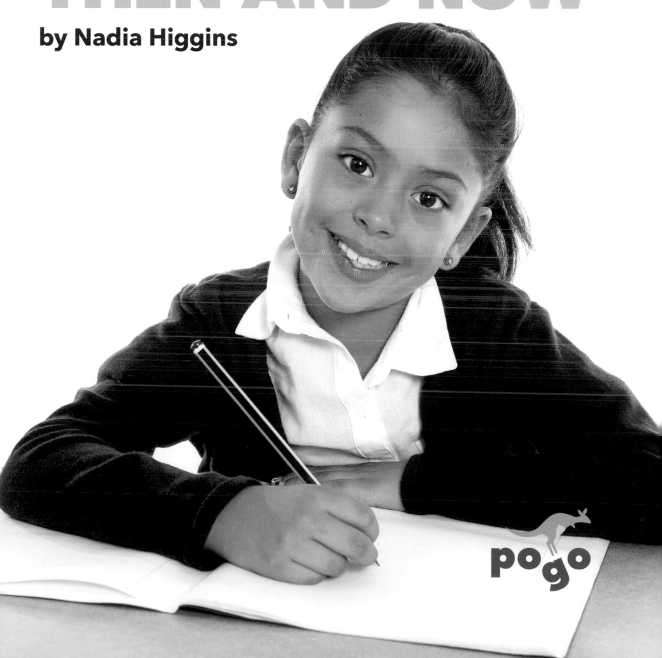

po**g**o

Ideas for Parents and Teachers

Pogo Books let children practice reading informational text while introducing them to nonfiction features such as headings, labels, sidebars, maps, and diagrams, as well as a table of contents, glossary, and index.

Carefully leveled text with a strong photo match offers early fluent readers the support they need to succeed.

Before Reading

- "Walk" through the book and point out the various nonfiction features. Ask the student what purpose each feature serves.
- Look at the glossary together. Read and discuss the words.

Read the Book

- Have the child read the book independently.
- Invite him or her to list questions that arise from reading.

After Reading

- Discuss the child's questions. Talk about how he or she might find answers to those questions.
- Prompt the child to think more. Ask: There are many forms of communication. What forms of communication do you use each day?

Pogo Books are published by Jump!
5357 Penn Avenue South
Minneapolis, MN 55419
www.jumplibrary.com

Library of Congress Cataloging-in-Publication Data

Names: Higgins, Nadia, author.
Title: Communication then and now / by Nadia Higgins.
Description: Minneapolis, MN: Pogo Books, [2019]
Series: Then and now | Includes index.
Identifiers: LCCN 2018030565 (print)
LCCN 2018049183 (ebook)
ISBN 9781641284707 (ebook)
ISBN 9781641284684 (hardcover : alk. paper)
ISBN 9781641284691 (pbk.)
Subjects: LCSH: Communication—History—Juvenile literature.
Classification: LCC P91.2 (ebook)
LCC P91.2 .H54 2019 (print) | DDC 302.2—dc23
LC record available at https://lccn.loc.gov/2018030565

Editor: Jenna Trnka
Designer: Molly Ballanger

Photo Credits: Andrey_Popov/Shutterstock, cover (left); David M. Schrader/Shutterstock, cover (right); OcusFocus/iStock, 1; Lev Kropotov/Shutterstock, 3 (left); Stephen B. Goodwin/Shutterstock, 3 (center); Sangaroon/Shutterstock, 3 (right); Kevin Dodge/Getty, 4; Legacy Images/Shutterstock, 5; Paul Doyle/Alamy, 6-7; Alamy, 8-9, 9; Jovanmandic/iStock, 10-11; whitemay/iStock, 12; Everett Historical/Shutterstock, 13; H. Armstrong Roberts/ClassicStock/Getty, 14-15; Lambert/Getty, 16-17; Comstock/Getty, 18; Bellurgent Jean Louis/Getty, 19; monkeybusinessimages/iStock, 20-21; McIninch/iStock, 23.

Printed in the United States of America at Corporate Graphics in North Mankato, Minnesota.

TABLE OF CONTENTS

CHAPTER 1

GET THE MESSAGE

A text. A smile. A billboard. What do these have in common? They are all ways to share a message. They are forms of **communication**.

petroglyph

Long ago, most Native Americans did not use written words. They told stories. They carved **petroglyphs** in rock. Even a drumbeat could carry news. Today, we still communicate with words, pictures, and **signals**.

In the 1600s, American **colonists** used **word of mouth** to spread news. The town crier shouted news in the street. Written **notices** were posted in town for all to see. People wrote letters by hand, too. Travelers passed them on.

DID YOU KNOW?

Before 1440, books were copied by hand. They took a long time to produce. They were expensive. Only rich people could buy them. But then the **printing press** changed the world. Books were less expensive to create. More people could afford them.

town crier

Printed newspapers began in the 1700s. Young children sold them in the streets. Big **headlines** shared exciting news.

WHAT DO YOU THINK?

How does your family get the news? By TV, radio, newspaper, or a website? What news do you get by word of mouth? How does each form change how you interpret the news?

NEWS

headline ····▶

The Boston Daily Globe.

BOSTON, TUESDAY EVENING, APRIL 16, 1912—TWENTY PAGES. PRICE TWO CENTS

EVENING EDITION—7:30 O'CLOCK

VOL. LXXXI—NO. 107.

ALL DROWNED BUT 868

About 1232 Lost Lives in the Titanic's Plunge, Greatest Sea Disaster for Years.

EXCITING EVENTS BEFORE TITANIC'S FINAL PLUNGE

Virginian and Parisian Found None A...

Women and Child... But Few Nota...

Carpathia Has ... On Way to ...

Only Partial List ... Owing to ...

BAY STAT...

In 1817, the American School for the Deaf opened. It was the first school to teach hand signs. Students shared their own signs, too. Over time, American Sign Language (ASL) developed. People who were deaf could fully communicate.

TAKE A LOOK!

To make an ASL sign, look at its three parts. Where is the hand placed? How is it shaped? How does it move? Try making these common signs.

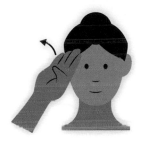

"HELLO"

"YOU'RE WELCOME"

"PLEASE"

"GOODBYE"

"THANK YOU"

"SORRY"

"YES"

"NO"

CHAPTER 2

FASTER AND FARTHER

For hundreds of years, a horse was the fastest way to carry a message. That changed around 1840. The **telegraph** sent news along wires. **Telegrams** were fast but expensive.

telegram

early
telephone

Telephones amazed the world in the 1870s. They used wires, too. But these wires carried voices. Now people could talk across miles.

radio ·····▶

Communication soon took another leap forward. The radio was invented in the 1890s. It did not use wires. Invisible waves carried voices through the air.

In the 1920s, radio stations popped up. They **broadcast** radio shows. Families gathered around their radios to listen to their favorite programs.

How do radio waves travel? Take a look!

LOCAL TOWER

③

TRANSMITTER

②

RADIO TOWER

①

MICROPHONE

RADIO

④

⑤

radio wave   sound wave

① **A microphone turns sound into electrical signals.**
② **A transmitter turns the signals to radio waves.**
③ **Radio waves travel at the speed of light to towers.**
④ **An antenna picks up the radio waves and turns them back into signals.**
⑤ **A radio turns the signals back into sound.**

By the 1950s, families gathered
around TVs instead of radios.
Video was put to words.
Americans viewed news
as it happened. In 1969,
they watched the first
astronauts walk on
the moon.

CHAPTER 3

SHIFT TO SCREENS

The 1990s saw a shift to screens. Families purchased computers. The Internet was growing.

People sent e-mails instead of letters. News was **published** online. E-books were available to read.

YOU'VE GOT MAIL!

early computer

early
cell phone

Cell phones were also on the rise. People used to have to make calls from home. Or they used public **pay phones**. Cell phones allow us to talk anywhere, anytime.

Communication keeps getting faster. It reaches more people. Think of all the ways you might connect with a friend. Talk face-to-face. Write a note. Call. E-mail. Text. Video chat. Post on **social media**. How do you communicate?

WHAT DO YOU THINK?

Today, we can communicate just about anywhere. On TVs, laptops, tablets, and phones. Some people say screens take up too much time. What do you think?

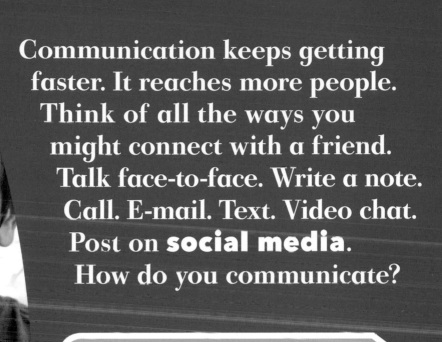

TRY THIS!

MAKE A SECRET CODE

A code is a system of signs, letters, or numbers that stand for words. Here are two ways to make up your own code. Use a code to communicate in secret with your friends.

① Mix Up Letters

Switch the order of letters, two by two.
A space counts as a letter.

TEXT ME
ETTXM E ↩

② Swap Out Letters

Write out the alphabet. For each letter, chose a symbol, letter, or number that will stand for it. This will be the key to your code.

A B C D E F G H I J K L M N O P Q R S T U V W X Y Z
9 $ J 4 X Q M 7 # E ! 3 6 L V S W T A 8 K Z % @ C R

TEXT ME
8X@8 6X ↩

broadcast: To send out a show or music on radio or TV.

colonists: The people who helped form the original 13 colonies of the United States.

communication: The sharing of information, ideas, or feelings with another person through written and spoken language, eye contact, or gestures.

headlines: The titles of newspaper, magazine, or web articles that appear in large, bold type.

notices: Pieces of news.

pay phones: Public phones that anyone can pay to use.

petroglyphs: Carvings in rock.

printing press: A large machine that prints words and designs by pressing sheets of paper against a surface, such as a metal plate, that has ink on it.

published: Produced and distributed for people to read.

signals: Sounds or actions that are used to communicate.

social media: Forms of electronic communication through which users create and share information.

telegrams: Messages sent by telegraph.

telegraph: A device or system for sending messages over long distances using a code of electrical signals sent by wire or radio.

word of mouth: Passing news from one person to another by speaking.

INDEX

TO LEARN MORE

Finding more information is as easy as 1, 2, 3.

1. Go to www.factsurfer.com
2. Enter "communicationthenandnow" into the search box.
3. Click the "Surf" button to see a list of websites.

FACT SURFER